Soul on
Paper

+ S K Candle
  penguin

+soulfulpenguin

ISBN: 978-0-578-76520-4

Cover Design: Anastasia Wingate-Piccolomini

Author & Illustrator: SKCooke

Instagram: @soulfulpenguin
Twitter: @_soulfulpenguin
Facebook: soulfulpenguin

To my father, the man who
taught me the value of words.

"In the end we both have
words that paint a page,
we put down on paper the
discussions we do not engage."
- JPCooke

I know you are painting
the clouds with your words.

Table of Contents

Strength & Perseverance

Love & the Heart

Hopes
& Beliefs

Beautiful Intentions

When you plant your
feet down in the morning,
I hope you do so
with the intention
of making every step
beautiful.

+soulfulpenguin – *4.5.2019*

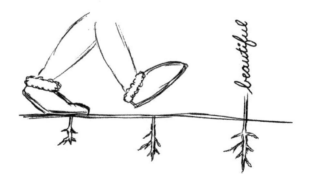

Changed by the Flames

I hope you find
what lights a fire
under your feet
because once you do
you'll never stand
the same again.

+soulfulpenguin – *6.14.2018*

doodle

Never Quit

She wasn't the most intelligent,
the strongest or the fastest,
but she had a drive
that made her the one
who would never quit.

+soulfulpenguin – *6.12.2017*

write

_____

_____

_____

_____

_____

_____

That Girl

She is the kind of girl you never forget,
the one who makes you feel like you can
dance on the moon, the one who changes
you with a smile, the one who strives for
more, the one whose heart grows by the
second.

She is the kind of girl you think only exists
in dreams and movies, the one who makes
you want to sprint past societal
boundaries, the one who gives you hope
for a new tomorrow and the one who
makes you a better you... today.

+soulfulpenguin – *9.25.2019*

Open Your Mind

Listen.
Before you get angry, listen.
For an angry heart
will give you a cold soul,
but an understanding ear
gives you the chance to
open your mind.

+soulfulpenguin – *4.5.2019*

imagine

Look for Rainbows

She believes in
seeing the good in people
and hoping they have
intentions of kindness.
Some may say
she is naïve
but she rather
find the rainbow
than stop searching
for beauty in a storm.

+soulfulpenguin – *5.23.2020*

Leave Pride & Ego at the Door

Speak with pure intentions
and listen with patient ears,
for communication
and compassion
will take you further
than your pride
and ego ever will.

+soulfulpenguin – *7.17.2019*

let it out

_____

_____

_____

_____

_____

_____

Nurturer

By nature,
she was a nurturer
as she felt most full
when she provided
for others.

+soulfulpenguin – *1.31.2019*

create

Kind to the Scars

Be kind to the scars of others,
as we haven't the clue
how deep the wound once was or
how easily it can be ripped open.

+soulfulpenguin – *1.27.2020*

think

———————————————

———————————————

———————————————

———————————————

———————————————

———————————————

Priceless are Those

Priceless are those
judgement-free people
who will be there for you
years after seeing them last,
with months between conversations,
and yet, always feel like home.

+soulfulpenguin – *6.15.2020*

Gifts

Be thankful
for the ones
who look out for you
without being asked
and expect
nothing in return.

+soulfulpenguin – *9.9.2019*

sketch

Judgement-Free to a Fault

I will never place
even a hair of judgement
when you tell me your story,
in fact I may be
a bit too understanding...
but if I fall short
by giving too much,
I'll know I did my best.

+soulfulpenguin – *3.17.2019*

mark it up

_____

_____

_____

_____

_____

_____

More Kind

I never want
to look back
and think
I could've been
more kind.

+soulfulpenguin – *3.12.2019*

make it yours

Peace, Love & Hope

Let's find peace
in the chaos and
love in our hearts,
for hope will be
on the horizon
if we lay low
and be smart.

+soulfulpenguin – *3.16.2020*

Silencing Solitude

She sang to the birds
in hopes they'd hear her chirps,
and sing along silencing
the sound of her solitude.

+soulfulpenguin – *12.10.2017*

breathe

_____

_____

_____

_____

_____

_____

_____

In Time's Hands

There is some sort of
power and peace
in knowing
you have done
all you can
and the rest
is up to time.

+soulfulpenguin – *6.10.2017*

scribble

A Reason

Maybe it won't make sense now
or for a while or maybe ever,
but there is a reason,
you must believe there is a reason,
as unbelievable as it may feel...
there is a reason.

+soulfulpenguin – *2.2.2019*

freewrite

_____

_____

_____

_____

_____

_____

Bridge to Your Dreams

When all seems lost
and you find yourself
at the end of the path,
worry not...
climb that tree and use it
as a bridge to your dreams.

+soulfulpenguin – *9.17.2020*

Glowing Too

Hope without end.
Act with intention.
Live with excitement.
When the sun rises,
you'll be glowing too.

+soulfulpenguin – *9.13.2020*

design

Radiant Soul

Be the type of person
that makes others feel
like the sun is shining strong
in the middle of the night.

+soulfulpenguin – *2.2.2019*

pen to paper

_____

_____

_____

_____

_____

_____

More Than Seasonal

She is the kind of girl that squishes
her toes in the sand, becoming one
with the shore... the kind of girl
that crunches on leaves as they fall
with the reflection of the most
vibrant oranges in her eyes...
the kind of girl that can withstand
the cold only because of the warmth
in her heart, and layers... lots of layers...
she is the kind of girl who gives
the most beautiful of flowers
competition but as she blossoms
there is truly no competition at all.

She is the kind of girl that
makes you count your blessings,
the one that makes you realize
every breath is a miracle,
the one that makes you hope
for endless tomorrows
filled with love and laughter
for life is too short for anything less.

+soulfulpenguin – *10.17.2019*

Wonder Eyes

No matter how old you get,
every day is a new one,
so even if your pockets
are full of wisdom,
I hope your eyes
remain full of wonder.

+soulfulpenguin – *7.7.2019*

make art

Let Them Go

Maybe some people
have to say goodbye
when they do,
for they have a
wonderful world
waiting for them
on the other side…
and we must
let them go,
but never forget.

+soulfulpenguin – *2.6.2019*

feel

_____

_____

_____

_____

_____

_____

Precious Life

Some days the
flowers don't bloom,
but your heart still beats
and that's all you need
to remind yourself how
precious this life is.

+soulfulpenguin – *10.21.2019*

draw

Tonight & Every Other

I hope you fall asleep tonight
with a heart full of love
and a belly full of calories
and remember all those
who took part in getting
the food to your table.

+soulfulpenguin – *11.22.2018*

A Step Forward

On the days you question
if you can keep going,
take a step for every obstacle
you have ever overcome
and you'll realize
you are a lot further
than you thought.

+soulfulpenguin – *1.27.2019*

think

_____

_____

_____

_____

_____

_____

_____

Superpower

Some days
it will storm
so hard
you lose
your electricity,
but that doesn't
mean you lose
your power.

+soulfulpenguin – *12.7.2018*

A Bit of Both

There were times
she fell face first
and moments
she conquered flawlessly
but in them both,
she lived... making her
past self proud and
her future self stronger.

+soulfulpenguin – *1.15.2019*

create

Stumble & Look Around

She challenged herself
to make light of every stumble,
so when her back was against
the cold, hard ground
she was able to look up
and see the blue of the sky,
feel the warmth of the sun,
and smile at the shapes
of the clouds.

+soulfulpenguin – *1.3.2019*

breathe

_____

_____

_____

_____

_____

Wind

She was inspired by the wind,
for its persistent strength
wasn't seen by the eye,
rather it was felt all around.

+soulfulpenguin – *1.29.2019*

What Reaches You

Let them throw sticks, stones, bricks and
boulders, for their arms will grow tired,
but you will remain untouched... for it is in
your power to choose what reaches you.

+soulfulpenguin – *8.29.2019*

make it yours

Worth Burning For

She grew from the flames
and found serenity in the waves
as she wiggled her toes into the sand
and learned not everyone
was worth burning for...

+soulfulpenguin – *8.31.2019*

let it out

_____

_____

_____

_____

_____

_____

_____

My Path

I will race no one
on the journey of life,
for my path looks
nothing like yours
and I'd like to
pick some flowers
on the way.

+soulfulpenguin – *5.6.2019*

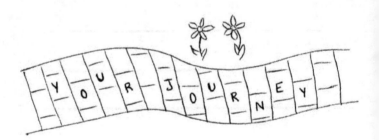

Irreplaceable Treasure

If you ever question your worth
let this be your reminder
that people are not born with price tags...
and you are irreplaceable treasure.

+soulfulpenguin – *6.28.2018*

design

Shine on Diamonds

A diamond is still a diamond no matter
how many times you drop it... so if anyone
comes close enough to dust you off,
make sure they respect your shine.

+soulfulpenguin – *7.11.2018*

note to self

_____

_____

_____

_____

_____

_____

Gem Friends

… and from that moment on
she decided to only
surround herself
with people who added
gems to her crown…

+soulfulpenguin – *9.11.2018*

The Ones

Gravitate towards the honest ones…
the ones who will tell you how it
really is for them, and truly want
to know how life is going for you…
the ones who you can laugh
at nothing with all through the night
and will be there to adventure
with you in the morning…
the ones that no matter the distance
or time, the core values of honesty,
trust and compassion are kept…
the ones that make you feel
the most like you.

+soulfulpenguin – *4.2.2019*

doodle

Believe in Me

Believe in me,
even when I stumble,
even when I fall.
Believe in me;
believe I'll
get back up
and keep going...
because I have before
and I will again.

+soulfulpenguin – *11.27.2018*

feel

———————————————

———————————————

———————————————

———————————————

———————————————

———————————————

Intuition

Let your intuition
be your compass
and your soul will
set sail with no plans
to look back.

+soulfulpenguin – *8.26.2019*

Go with Your Tide

If the tide of your soul
takes you out to sea,
don't let the wind of others
push you back to shore.

+soulfulpenguin – *2.15.2019*

imagine

Keep Fighting

Keep fighting,
because you've
made it this far.
Keep fighting,
because it may be
your only choice.
Keep fighting,
because it may be
your last chance.

+soulfulpenguin – *12.3.2018*

pour it out

_____

_____

_____

_____

_____

_____

Some Days

Some days it's about
productivity and efficiency.
Some days it's about
happiness and love.
Some days it's about
hard work and progression.

Some days it's about all of the above.

Some days it's simply about
getting through the day...
and knowing that even if
everything isn't going right...
you are still going to be okay.

+soulfulpenguin – *10.9.2017*

scribble

Crumbling

There will be days the world
feels so very heavy...
and it is on those days
you must recognize
the strength you possess...
and it is on those days
you must take an extra minute
to break off a piece of yourself
and allow it to crumble,
for you are human and
what beautiful growth
comes with crumbling.

+soulfulpenguin – *1.16.2020*

journal

_____

_____

_____

_____

_____

_____

Spin On

Her life played like a record
and she knew a scratch or two
was expected over time,
but she spun on
making beautiful music
for all of her days.

+soulfulpenguin – *3.18.2019*

Imperfect but Complete

He was far from perfect,
but he lived completely
for as long as he was
given the chance.

+soulfulpenguin – *11.11.2017*

draw

Your Ascent

When the mountain
seems too big to climb,
that's when the view
will be worth it.

Let no one stop your ascent.

+soulfulpenguin – *7.31.2017*

Effort & Prayers

Have big dreams and crazy goals
and when the moon shines
on your face and the waves splash
on your toes, you'll know
it was effort and prayers
that got you through your woes.

+soulfulpenguin – *6.3.2019*

mark it up

_____

_____

_____

_____

_____

_____

Stronger from the Venture

As the light dimmed,
she remembered dark times
she had once lived through
and knew this was just
another venture that would
make her stronger.

+soulfulpenguin – *12.2.2018*

make art

Cut the Ties

Those who choose to hang on
to the stones of troubles past
will carry a load that will never
allow their feet to leave the ground…
but if you want to let your dreams
take you beyond the clouds,
you must learn to cut the ties and fly.

+soulfulpenguin – *11.19.2017*

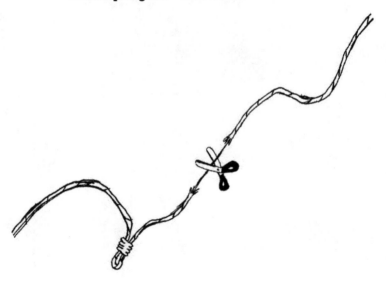

Let Go for Your Future

You'll find peace in letting go...
some things are better left in
the past and darling,
you have no idea how bright
your future can be.

+soulfulpenguin – *2.23.2020*

pen to paper

_____

_____

_____

_____

_____

_____

_____

Growing Glory

… and you keep growing,
for you are not the seed
or even the little bud
you once were,
so stay watering,
but don't forget
to let your petals
feel the sun and
appreciate the glory
at every stage.

+soulfulpenguin – *8.28.2019*

sketch

Loves You Harder

I hope you
love you
as you deserve
and then
find someone
who loves you
even harder
than that.

+soulfulpenguin – *1.3.2020*

Wants

I think we all want butterflies
and the life that lives beyond them...
like the blessing to have a human
by your side on days that test
your patience and the nights
your mind is marathon running.

I think we all want cute dates,
like a picnic in the park and
movies with cuddles after dark...
but only with someone whose
love has no expiration.

I think we all want happiness,
but to share it with someone who
stays for the struggles of sadness
and moments where hope is hidden.

I think we all want love, but the kind
that comes with no tally marks of errors
or arguments, the kind that makes
you feel alive and free, the kind that
loves you in all stages.

+soulfulpenguin – *9.18.2020*

Her Language

He is mysterious and hard to read...
but when he is interested
he makes sure to speak her language.

+soulfulpenguin – *9.18.2020*

write

_____

_____

_____

_____

_____

_____

_____

Forever Changed

Little did I know that
from the moment
my eyes met yours,
part of my soul would be
forever changed...

+soulfulpenguin – *6.11.2019*

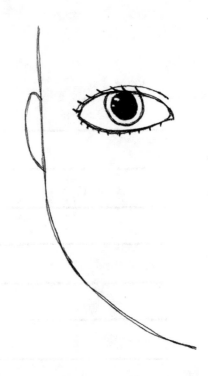

Human Desires

She soon realized
voicing her desires
didn't make her needy,
for they made her human…
and "human"
is a good thing to be.

+soulfulpenguin – *4.4.2017*

imagine

Letting Loose

He made her feel like
her "crazy" was nothing to hide
and so she rolled down the windows,
let her hair loose and played the song
of her heart for all of the world to hear.

+soulfulpenguin – *4.24.2018*

breathe

_____

_____

_____

_____

_____

_____

_____

Beautiful Little Details

Those little details of yourself
you pick apart...
are so damn beautiful...
they make you, perfectly you...
and I bet someone loves you
even more for them.

+soulfulpenguin – *1.29.2020*

make it yours

Make Her Laugh

Make her laugh,
and if you
fall in love
with the way
her eyes squint
and you
admire
the beauty
in her
jumbled
words
as she
floats into
a state
of delirium,
then never stop
making her laugh.

+soulfulpenguin – *5.8.2018*

Flying

.. and we laughed so hard
for so long we had forgotten
what started it all...
and in that moment
I felt like I was flying...

+soulfulpenguin – *4.8.2019*

feel

_____

_____

_____

_____

_____

_____

_____

There's You

There's nothing quite like
waking to slightly dewy grass
and the sun peeking through the trees
with the smell of sweet flowers and
the aroma of fresh coffee filling the air...
but then again there's you.

+soulfulpenguin – *9.16.2020*

Knotted Together

Don't tell me you
think I'm perfect.
        Tell me you know
        there are knots in my rope
        and tell me you will be there
        while I untangle them and
                help me when I look like
                I am ready to give up
                on myself.

        +soulfulpenguin – *9.20.2018*

scribble

Dissipate the Distance

Sometimes it isn't about
what you say or
how much you say it...
sometimes it's about
just being there to
dissipate the distance.

+soulfulpenguin – *1.17.2019*

pour it out

_____

_____

_____

_____

_____

_____

_____

Incredible & Perfect

At the end of the day we want
something incredible that will last
with our perfect one…
but to even come close to this
we must understand that no human
is perfect, and not every moment
will be incredible but to have a love
that lasts through the big moments
and little moments, through the
tough times and wonderful times
is more incredible and perfect
than we could even wish for.

+soulfulpenguin – *1.2.2020*

freehand

Love, Communication & Compromise

It's not about who wears the pants...
it's about love, communication and
compromise... realizing that
you each need to take a leg
to walk this life together.

+soulfulpenguin – *8.3.2019*

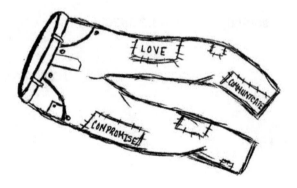

Busy Bee with a Big Heart

He is always a busy bee,
buzzing about his day,
but he never forgets
to let her know his heart
beats for her.

+soulfulpenguin – *7.25.2018*

freewrite

—————————————————

—————————————————

—————————————————

—————————————————

—————————————————

—————————————————

—————————————————

Worlds Tied Together

Hearing about your day
is the best part of mine.
Not because I don't
have my own world
within this universe,
but because in those
moments we are tying
our worlds tightly together.

+soulfulpenguin – *12.5.2018*

draw

Safe Place

Be their safe place,
the one they can come to
when their walls have crumbled
and dust has filled the sky.
Be the one to hold them tight
and remind them darkness
has a purpose too.

+soulfulpenguin – *10.7.2019*

Chooses to Stay

She wants someone
that chooses to be
by her side
in the happiest
of moments and
only presses his feet
further in the ground
during the moments
of struggle and defeat.

+soulfulpenguin – *6.10.2019*

mark it up

_____

_____

_____

_____

_____

_____

Calm Me & Love Me Harder

Calm me when I am a storm
and love me harder
when my frustrations
cloud the view of the
sunshine in my world.

+soulfulpenguin – *10.21.2018*

Loved Her Tighter

Some days, he held her tighter.
He didn't want to let one moment go by
with her feeling any less than loved.

+soulfulpenguin – *11.28.2017*

doodle

Beautiful & Enough

He is always there
to remind her
that her best
is good enough
and even on
the ugly days,
she is still beautiful.

+soulfulpenguin – *3.29.2018*

pen to paper

_____

_____

_____

_____

_____

_____

_____

Such Power

She believes
in the power
of fireflies
and lullabies
and that
true love
lasts through
blue and
gray skies.

+soulfulpenguin – *6.24.2018*

In the Morning

She always tried to follow the
"don't go to bed angry" rule
but despite his unwillingness to abide,
she promised to always be there
in the morning.

+soulfulpenguin – *8.17.2018*

sketch

My Intention

I promise you this,
my intention
is never to be
up against you...
only right beside.

+soulfulpenguin – *3.18.2019*

let it out

——————————————————

——————————————————

——————————————————

——————————————————

——————————————————

——————————————————

Undoubtable Love

I don't need a grand gesture;
I need undoubtable love.

+soulfulpenguin – *5.4.2019*

make art

Let's Stay in Bed

Let's stay in bed all day
covered in blankets and kisses,
forgetting the concept of time
and the world outside our door.

+soulfulpenguin – *2.6.2019*

Love You More

All my heart wants to do
is love you until you feel it
in every cell of your existence
and even then, it will only
crave to love you more.

+soulfulpenguin – *3.5.2019*

journal

_____

_____

_____

_____

_____

_____

_____

What's Love to You?

I would cross oceans
to make your life
even an ounce
easier in a blink...
because to me
that's love.

+soulfulpenguin – *8.18.2019*

create

Lasting Love

She didn't need a fairytale ending;
she needed love that lasted
through the moments that were
anything but a storybook.

+soulfulpenguin – *2.3.2019*

Day In & Out

I want someone who will laugh
deliriously with me at the end
of long crazy days or come to me
crying if that's what feels right.

I want someone I can turn to
when I feel the world crumbling
and have him know I'll always
be there to help build him up
when he feels rock bottom
beneath his feet.

I want someone who isn't afraid
to tell me when he is mad,
but will respect me endlessly
no matter his mood.

I want someone that knows life
isn't perfect and neither are we,
but still be that someone
who wants to live through
this life together...
side by side...
day in and out.

+soulfulpenguin – *6.24.2020*

My Person

There is no one
I would rather conquer
every adventure of life
with but you...
and that's how I know
you're my person.

+soulfulpenguin – *5.25.2019*

think

_____

_____

_____

_____

_____

_____

Best Friend & True Love

Fall in love with
your best friend
and you'll find
every day you
fall in love
all over again.

+soulfulpenguin – *8.26.2019*

design

Never Grow Old

She knows with him
she will age,
but never grow old.

+soulfulpenguin – *10.20.2017*

First Day

I hope when we're old
and gray we smile
at each other
like the very first day...

+soulfulpenguin – *5.7.2020*

note to self

_____

_____

_____

_____

_____

_____

_____

"To Be Continued"

Our love story
will forever be a
"to be continued."

+soulfulpenguin – *2.2.2018*

CPSIA information can be obtained
at www.ICGtesting.com
Printed in the USA
FSHW020004040121
77362FS